Robbie and his Merry Men

MICHAELA MORGAN

Illustrated by Doffy Weir

And us!

OXFORD
UNIVERSITY PRESS

OXFORD
UNIVERSITY PRESS

Great Clarendon Street, Oxford OX2 6DP

Oxford University Press is a department of the University of Oxford.
It furthers the University's objective of excellence in research, scholarship,
and education by publishing worldwide in

Oxford   New York

Auckland   Cape Town   Dar es Salaam   Hong Kong   Karachi
Kuala Lumpur   Madrid   Melbourne   Mexico City   Nairobi
New Delhi   Shanghai   Taipei   Toronto

With offices in

Argentina   Austria   Brazil   Chile   Czech Republic   France   Greece
Guatemala   Hungary   Italy   Japan   Poland   Portugal   Singapore
South Korea   Switzerland   Thailand   Turkey   Ukraine   Vietnam

Oxford is a registered trade mark of Oxford University Press
in the UK and in certain other countries

British Library Cataloguing in Publication Data
Data available

ISBN-13: 978-0-19-917997-8
ISBN-10: 0-19-917997-2

5 7 9 10 8 6 4

Available in packs
Stage 12 Pack of 6:
ISBN-13: 978-0-19-917993-0; ISBN-10: 0-19-917993-X
Stage 12 Class Pack:
ISBN-13: 978-0-19-919968-6; ISBN-10: 0-19-919968-X
Guided Reading Cards also available:
ISBN-13: 978-0-19-919970-9; ISBN-10: 0-19-919970-1

Cover artwork by Doffy Weir
Photograph of Michaela Morgan © Richard Drewe

Printed by Ashford Colour Press

Chapter 1

I'm Robbie Woods.

I'm always the first to make a good joke.

I'm always the first to tidy my work away at the end of the day.

But somehow I'm never the first to be picked for teams and plays.

Big Bradley Tomlinson and Bossy Becky Sparrow always get to pick the teams for rounders.

'I'll have Jack and Scott and Jordan and Sam,' says Big Bradley.

'I'll have Carly and Kylie and Katy and Kaylee,' says Bossy Becky.

5

It's the same with the school play.

In my first year at school,
we did the Christmas
Nativity Play.

No, I wasn't Joseph.

I wasn't a Wise Man either.

I wasn't a shepherd.

I was a sheep.

I had to stand there
looking woolly and
being quiet.

I wasn't even allowed to go 'Baaaa'.

The next year, we did Humpty
Dumpty.

No, I wasn't Humpty Dumpty.
That was Katy.

I wasn't one of the King's Men.
They were Becky, Jack, and Scott.

I wasn't one
of the King's
Horses either.

I was a brick in the wall.
I just had to stand there, wearing
a box and then fall over.

Oh
ROBBIE!

BEANS
BEANS
BEANS
BEANS

The next year, we did the Pied Piper.

No, I wasn't the Pied Piper. That was Jordan (because he can play the recorder).

I wasn't the Mayor. That was Bradley (because he's big).

I wasn't one of the townsfolk and I wasn't one of the children.

I was a rat.

This time I had words to learn and say. It was what they call a 'speaking part'. I had to say — squeak squeak squeak squeak

If you ask me it was more of a squeaking part than a speaking part.

Chapter 2

Our teacher, Miss Goody, called everyone together.

This year our play will be the story of Robin Hood and his Merry Men.

'What about his merry women?' said Becky. 'It's sexist!'

'What about his miserable men?' said Scott. 'It's miserablist!'

'What about just getting on with it,' said Miss Goody. 'Who would like to be Robin Hood?'

I shot my hand up into the air.

I would!

'Robbie Woods would...' said Miss Goody.

'Robbie Woods would. Robbie Woods would, would he...' Bradley began to chant.

But I ignored him. 'I'm dead keen on Robin Hood,' I explained.

'I know all the stories.

I've got all the books.

I've got a bow and arrow.

I've even got my own Robin Hood costume,' I said.

'But *I* want to be Robin Hood,' said Becky.

'And me!' said Bradley.

'I will give everyone a chance,' said Miss Goody. 'There are all these parts.'

Robin Hood   Maid Marian
Little John   Friar Tuck
The Sheriff of Nottingham
The Minstrel ,   Allan a Dale
Will Scarlet

'And there are also parts for villagers, knights, and ladies... and of course we'll need lots and lots of trees to be the forest.'

I can guess what I'm going to be.

Chapter 3

'I bet I'll be a tree,' I sighed.

'No you won't,' said Becky. 'You'll be a little baby bush…'

'Or a teeny tiny twig,' said Bradley.

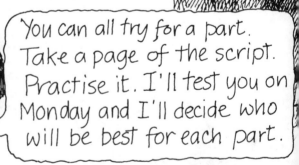

'Quiet,' said Miss Goody.

You can all try for a part. Take a page of the script. Practise it. I'll test you on Monday and I'll decide who will be best for each part.

I took a copy of the Robin Hood words.

Robin Hood (boldly)	Good morrow lords and ladies I am bold Robin Hood. I fight the foe with sword so bright And live in the Greenwood.

Forsooth I am a proud outlaw A proud outlaw I be, I rob the rich to feed the poor And sleep under the greenwood tree. |
| Maid Marian | *Mm I mmm mmmc mmm mmm you I said mmmm mmm mmm mm* |
| Friar Tuck | *mmm's mm a mmmmmm mmm mm m amm mmm mmm mmm mm mm mm m m. mmm m m mm mm.* |

There were lots of words.
And some of them were a bit strange.

Forsooth?!

But I was determined
to be Robin Hood.

I mean, if your name was Frankie Stein, you'd be interested in Frankenstein. Wouldn't you?

If your name was Richard King, you'd be interested in King Richard. Wouldn't you?

And my name, Robbie Woods, is just like Robin Hood. So it's only natural I'd take an interest in a hero with the same name (almost) as me. Isn't it?

I'm not the only one to notice how like Robin Hood I am.

All my uncles and aunties give me Robin Hood presents.

I've got Robin Hood teddies (I've had those since I was little).

I've got Robin Hood jigsaws (and it's not easy doing a jigsaw which is nearly all green).

green trees

green hat

green clothes

green bushes

JIGSAW

green grass

sky (not green)

I've got all the videos of all the Robin Hood films and... I've got cassettes of Robin Hood songs.

I made up my own version. I'd gallop round the playground (when I was little) singing:

Robbie Woods, Robbie Woods
and his Merry Men
Robbie Woods, Robbie Woods
Here he comes again.
Feared by the bad,
Loved by the good,
Robbie Woods, Robbie Woods,
Robbie Woods.

There were other versions, mostly made up by Bradley but I didn't like those so much:

Robbie Woods, Robbie Woods
running round the school.
Robbie Woods, Robbie Woods
Looking like a fool.
Feared by the sad,
Loved by the girls,
Robbie Woods, Robbie Woods,
Robbie Woods.

But I don't care if Bradley teases. I want to play the part of Robin Hood. Trouble is – so does Bradley.

Chapter 4

Bradley is clever.

Very clever.

Give him words to learn and before you can say

ABRACADABRA

or SHAZAM

or even YOU WHAT?

he's learnt them.

I have to try a bit harder. But I took the script and decided I would learn it by Monday.

I read the words
on the way home.

I spoke them out loud and clear.

I practised the actions.

At teatime I practised.

At bathtime I practised.

At bedtime I practised.
All the next day I practised.

It was hard. I kept forgetting things
and making mistakes but I didn't give up.

On Monday while everyone was out for playtime I got my chance to try for the part.

'Take your time. Take a deep breath. Don't be nervous,' said Miss Goody.

And I did it.

I spoke very loud and very clear.

I did some brilliant acting and I remembered every word.

I got the part.

'You really learnt the part well,' said
Miss Goody.

Pages
and pages
and pages
of it.

Chapter 5

Bradley got the part of Little John. He got that part because he's the biggest in the class. He still really wanted to be Robin Hood.

'Can't wait for our swordfight scene,' he said.

Then we'll see who's the real hero.

Becky would have loved to be Robin Hood but she would also have been happy to be Little John. Instead she was one of the ladies-in-waiting. She had to smile a lot and say, 'Yes, my lady.'

Jordan was the minstrel. He didn't want to be in the play at all but Miss Goody insisted.

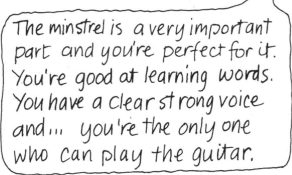

The minstrel is a very important part and you're perfect for it. You're good at learning words. You have a clear strong voice and... you're the only one who can play the guitar.

I'd always thought a minstrel was a chocolate sweet but it turns out it's someone who tells stories and sings songs. The minstrel in our story was the narrator. He told the tale in song with a little strum of the guitar every now and then.

He had lots of words to learn.

Of course the biggest and best part was the part of Robin Hood. Everybody wanted that part but I'd got it.

A STAR AT LAST

'You'll never learn all that,' said Bradley.

Why don't you give up now?

But I was determined to be the best Robin Hood ever. I've got the part of a hero and a hero I shall be.

I had three weeks to learn it. It was hard.

I practised in the park. My friends helped.

I practised in the supermarket. My mum helped.

26

I practised all the way to school. The lollipop lady helped.

Here's a river I have to cross but who stands in my way?

I'm Little John and I'm the boss. You can't cross here today.

Even Becky helped me. She was bored being a lady-in-waiting so she rehearsed with me. She played Little John's part and gave me hints on fighting.

But I still got nervous when everyone (especially Bradley) was watching. They seemed to be waiting for me to make mistakes. And I made plenty of them.

Here come I, Robbie Hood, with my Merry Rubber Band.

ROBBER BAND!

The more mistakes I made. The more nervous I got. The more nervous I made. The more nervous I got. The more mistakes I made the more nervous

I felt dizzy with worry.

Jitters

COLLY

Miss Goody took me to one side.

'Robbie,' she said. 'Are you a bit worried about the play?'

A bit worried?

Oh no...

Sometimes I was hot and bothered.
Sometimes I was in a cold sweat.

shivers ~ **heebie**

I had knocking knees, cold feet, and
goose pimples big as goose eggs.

WOBBLES ~ **shakes** **jeebies**

I had shaky hands, wobbly legs
and butterflies big as seagulls in my
tummy.

But I wasn't a BIT worried.

I was TERRIFIED!!

But I was still determined to
be Robin Hood.

Chapter 6

At home I did my best to practise, but since Grandad came to live with us we don't have a lot of spare room.

I got a great echo practising in the bathroom but no one was very keen on me practising in there.

Await, forsooth
I clean my tooth

Hurry up Robbie!

I want my potty!

Forsooth!

Then Grandad said, 'You can practise in my shed. That's the place for peace and quiet.'

The shed is where Grandad keeps all the piles of stuff he brought with him when Grandma died. He's got boxes and boxes of bits and bobs that he says will come in useful.

He and Mum came down and cleared a space for me.

'If I move this box you can sit down here,' said Mum. 'Oh… look at that! It's your old banjo. You used to love playing that.'

'Play me a tune, Grandad,' I said.

But he just sighed. 'It's not the same without your Grandma,' he said. 'She used to love to hear me play.'

'But we'd love to hear you play, wouldn't we?' Mum nudged me. She'd been trying to cheer Grandad up for ages.

'Yes,' I said.

Why don't you help me with the minstrel scenes? You can sing his words and play the banjo.

'It would really help him,' said my mum.

Oh, all right....

Grandad gave the banjo a half-hearted twang.

plink   plonk

After half an hour there was no stopping him.

He was singing louder and louder, stomping his feet and playing faster and faster and he was really getting into the minstrel's part. He even made up a minstrel dance.

We practised every day. He really cheered up and so did I. It made learning the words much easier and funny.

I got an extra ticket for the play. I had a feeling that Grandad would want to see it.

stomp
stomp

At school the rehearsals were going better. I was remembering my words quite well, but it was hard acting with Bradley especially in that fighting-to-get-across-the-river scene. He would always shout that little bit too loud.

He would slap my back that little bit too often.

And he would always push that little bit too hard.

In the final dress rehearsal he was really getting carried away. He was waving his stick round and round in the air.

'Careful, Bradley,' said Miss Goody.

He was shouting louder and louder and pushing harder and harder until...

...he lost his balance and fell off the bridge.

OW! My ankle!

He had sprained his ankle.

'You won't be able to stand on that ankle for tonight's performance,' said Miss Goody.

Ouch!

'Will we have to cancel the play?' asked Becky.

Carly started to cry.
Kylie joined in.
Then Kaylee started.
They always did everything together. You'd think they were triplets.

WAAAH!!

They wailed and sobbed and sobbed and wailed. Miss Goody tried to make things better. 'Nobody blames you, Bradley,' she said, 'so stop sulking. And Carly and Company will you stop that noise. I can't think.'

Can *anybody else* learn the part....... before tonight?

She looked at a group of boys.

| Scott shrugged. | Sam shook his head. | Jack shuffled his feet. |

Miss Goody sighed. Everyone sighed. It was just not possible to learn the words and the actions in the time.

Then Becky stood up.
'What about
me?' she said.

I've practised the part
with Robbie. I've been to
all the rehearsals. I could
do it really well. And
Carly could have my part
as lady-in-waiting.

Carly stopped crying in mid sniff.
'Could I?' she said.

Miss Goody
stopped
frowning.

I sighed
with relief.

Everyone cheered.

Carly and Co burst into tears of joy.

'That only leaves one problem,' said the secretary, coming in with a phone message.

Jordan, the minstrel. He's got the measles.

'Oh no!' said Bradley.
'Oh no!' said Becky.
'OH NO!!!' said everyone else except Carly and Co who were crying fit to bust. And now Becky was joining in and so was Jack. Even Bradley was getting a bit of a red nose.

Sniff

Waaa!

Sob....

I didn't feel too happy myself.
After all I'd been through I wouldn't be able to be Robin Hood.

After all that practising in the park.

After all that reading in my bed and after all that rehearsing with my grandad as the min...

But we phoned Grandad and he
came to school.

| He showed how he knew all the words. | And he showed how well he played the banjo. |

He danced his mad minstrel dance
and everyone agreed he was brilliant.
He glowed with pride.
Miss Goody sighed with relief
and I felt... like a hero.

Goody
goody!

In the performance that night he
was nearly perfect.

He just made one mistake. He kept
saying Robbie Woods instead of Robin
Hood. I liked it.

And everyone clapped
and clapped
and clapped.

About the author

I've written about fifty
stories for children.

I work at home and start
by making little, blotty
notes on odd scraps of
paper. Then I type it on my
computer. I put it in my
drawer and take it out
from time to time to make
changes. Each time I work on it,
it gets a little bit better, until eventually,
I feel ready to send it to a publisher.

Then, the publisher makes it into a book
like this, for you to read and enjoy.